THE BOOK OF FANTASTIC MACHINES

Illustrated by
KEN RUSH

Written by
JEAN RUSH

Copyright © 1974 The Archon Press Limited, London
U.S. edition published 1974 by Golden Press, New York. Western Publishing Company, Inc. Printed in U.S.A.
All rights reserved. Golden, A Golden Book ®, and Golden Press ® are trademarks of Western Publishing Company, Inc.
Library of Congress Catalog Card Number: 73-92283
ISBN: 0 307 12675 7

GOLDEN PRESS · NEW YORK
Western Publishing Company, Inc.
Racine, Wisconsin

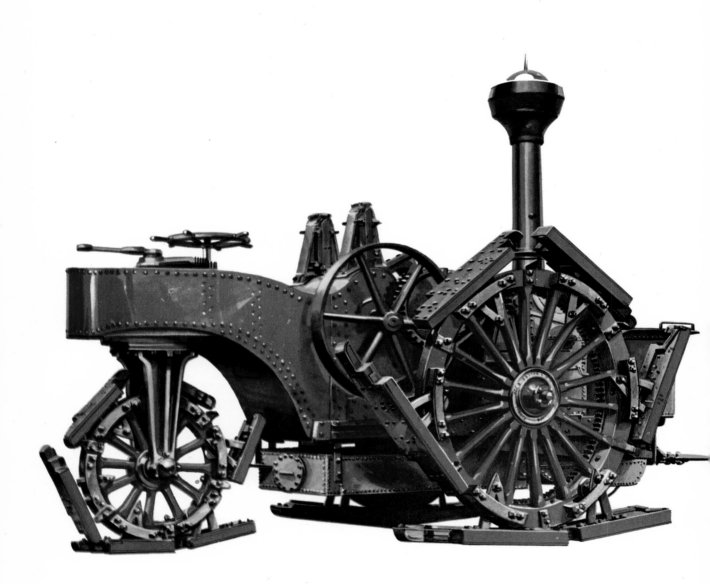

INTRODUCTION

Modern man's distant ancestors, the men of the Stone Ages, had only wood, stone and bone out of which to fashion their tools. Neolithic man, the man of the New Stone Age, made stone lamps which he filled with animal fat for lighting. He invented sewing needles so that he was able to make clothes out of the skins of animals. And he fished with hooks and hunted with arrows.

In time, Neolithic man left the caves which had been his home. He built huts and erected great stone monuments to his gods. He became a farmer as well as a hunter. He grew crops of barley and learned how to make flour from which he baked bread. He drank the beer he made from his barley, too. And eventually he began to domesticate animals.

The inventions of Neolithic man made many of these changes and developments possible. There seemed to be no end to his ingenuity. When he grew weary of tools that were awkward to handle, he invented others that worked easier. When man discovered metals in the earth, he set about inventing even more new kinds of tools. Metal axes appeared along with metal ploughshares.

Over the centuries, man slowly made simple tools into machines. The plough gave way to all kinds of agricultural appliances, and the wheel made possible an endless range of devices and machines. The more knowledge man gained, the more complex and ambitious became his machines.

For centuries this process of machine development has continued, and this book includes some of the most fascinating machines invented over the last 250 years. They have been selected because they were the first machines of their kind and were often landmarks in engineering history. Two of the machines shown are concerned with 19th century man's deep longing to fly like a bird. Others are testimonies to man's determination to harness steam to machines of his own creation. Also included are some 'firsts': the first bicycle, the earliest pocket sewing machine, the first gramophone, the first robot to land on the moon.

Some words that may be unfamiliar are explained in the glossary at the back of this book.

PUCKLE
MACHINE GUN
1718

Country: Great Britain. **Size:** 3 ft.
10 in. high, barrel 2 ft. 11 in. long.
It was the first machine gun.

James Puckle, a Sussex lawyer, invented a machine that was
to change the course of history. It was very similar to the
Gatling gun which came into use more than 1½ centuries later.
Attached to the single barrel was a revolving disc which held a set of
chambers, each containing a charge of powder. With each turn, the locking
handle received a chamber onto the barrel, and the charge was fired by a
flintlock mechanism. Labelling it 'a portable gun or machine called a
defense,' Puckle demonstrated his gun to the Ordnance Board. They were
not impressed, and although he did his best to sell his idea, it never went
into service.

HARRISON'S CHRONOMETER 1735

Country: Great Britain. **Size:** 2 ft. high × 2 ft. wide and 72 lbs.
It was the first reliable timekeeping device at sea.

Until the introduction of the chronometer in the mid-18th century,
navigation was by the stars (a method which was not wholly reliable).
The chronometer is a timekeeping instrument which remains completely
accurate under varying conditions at sea. Looking like a clock with many
dials, the chronometer was suspended in such a way that it stayed hori-
zontal however violent the movement of the ship. By comparing the exact
time on the dials with the position of the sun, the captain could work out his
accurate position. John Harrison was the inventor of this first reliable
chronometer.

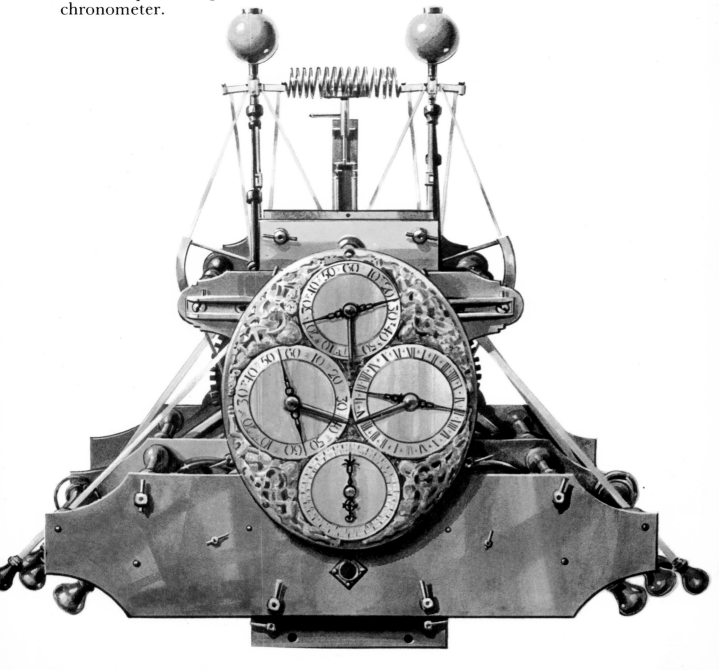

CAYLEY'S AERIAL CARRIAGE 1843

Country: Great Britain. **Size:** 20 ft. long, disc 11 ft. 3 in. in diameter.
It was a design for a convertiplane.

Sir George Cayley, a wealthy Yorkshire baronet, was a true inventor in the history of flight, and in 1804 produced the world's first aircraft—a model glider. This was followed by a rush of new and successful inventions, including the first manned glider in 1853. The aerial carriage you see below was a design for a convertiplane (a combination of helicopter and plane). The circular discs were to provide the lift to get the craft airborne, while at the same time the pressure of the air rotated these discs to drive the propellers at the back. Just how far Cayley experimented with his design is not recorded but it is known that life was not easy for the staff of this remarkable inventor. His coachman, who flew in the first manned glider in 1853, is reputed to have said on landing, 'Please, Sir George, I wish to give notice, I was not hired to fly!'

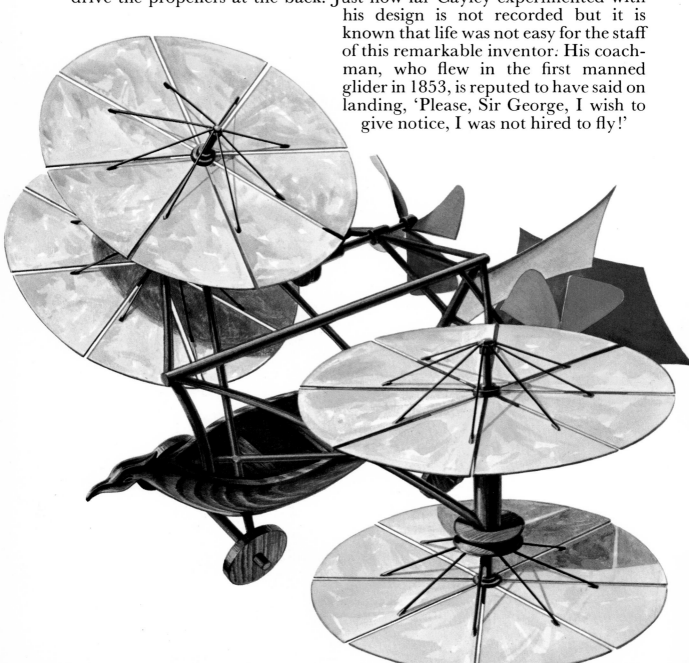

NATURAL FLYING MACHINE
1865

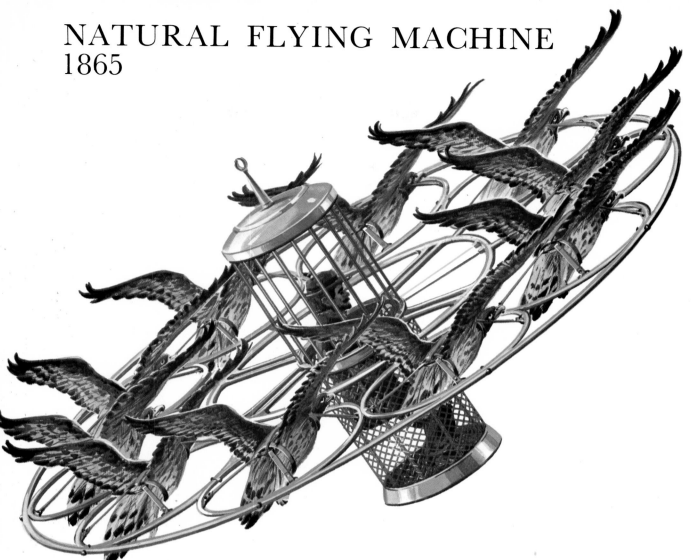

Country: United States. **Size:** approx. 6 ft. high, 19 ft. across.
It was one of the most ingenious Natural Flying Machines.

Throughout the ages men used animals to carry them on land, but when it came to the air, they always failed. It frustrated many inventors to realize that though birds could fly so effortlessly, there seemed to be no way in which they could help man to do the same. The idea of the Natural Flying Machine, more imaginative than most, came from a Baltimore inventor whose name is not known. His machine was a circular framework of hollow tubes, carrying a metal basket large enough to hold a man. Ten brown eagles, chosen for their strong wings and ability to fly long distances, were harnessed to the contraption by cords passing through the tubes. The 'pilot' was intended to control his height with these cords, by compressing or releasing the eagles' wings, and he was to steer by moving the heads of the birds in a similar way. Needless to say, this Natural Flying Machine was a failure, and it isn't known whether the inventor tried it out himself or, like Cayley, took advantage of his coachman!

SUTHERLAND
STEAM FIRE ENGINE 1863

Country: Great Britain. **Size:** approx. 8 ft. long, 5 ft. high.
It is the oldest steam fire engine in existence.

Steam power (which was invented almost 100 years before) was not applied to fire fighting until 1829. Strangely, it took another 30 years before the steam fire engine was in general use. The Sutherland, pictured here, is believed to be the oldest steam fire engine still in existence. Built by the Merryweathers Co., it won first prize at an international fire-fighting competition held at the Crystal Palace in London. This early steam fire engine was horse-drawn, and the steam engine was used only to drive the pump, which was able to throw a powerful jet of water over 160 feet.

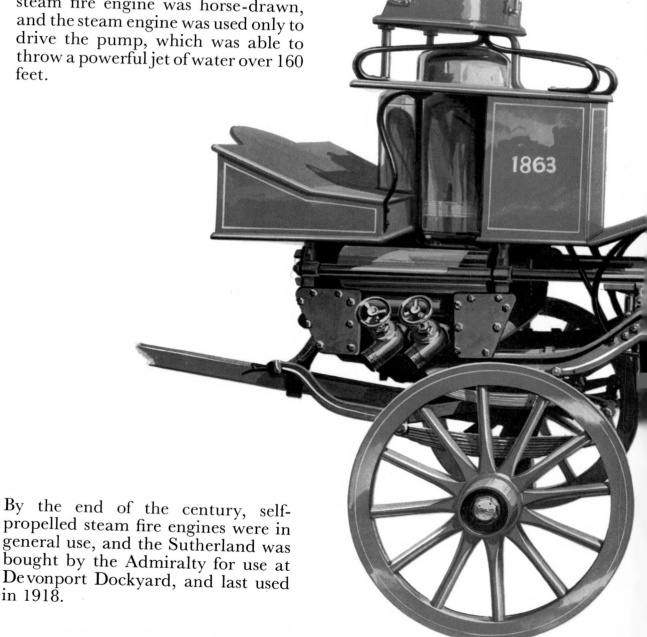

By the end of the century, self-propelled steam fire engines were in general use, and the Sutherland was bought by the Admiralty for use at Devonport Dockyard, and last used in 1918.

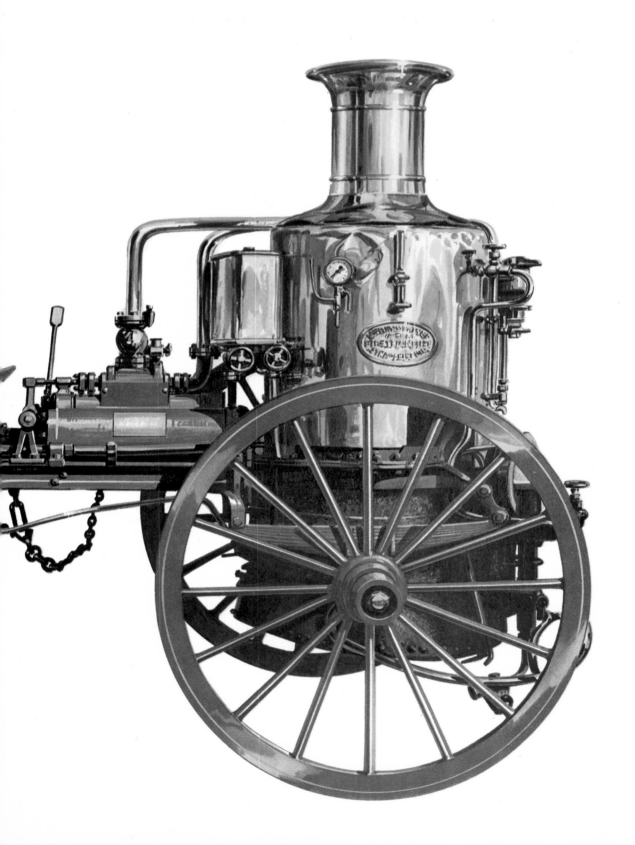

TUXFORD'S BOYDELL TRACTION ENGINE 1858

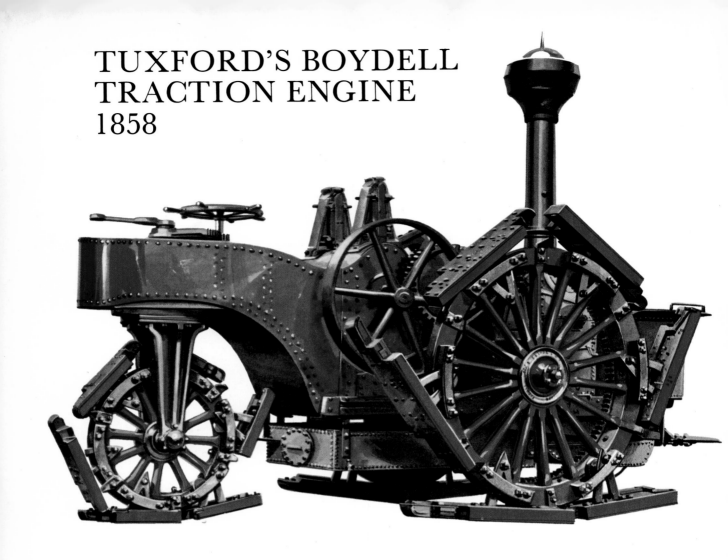

Country: Great Britain. **Size:** 17–18 ft. long, 13–14 ft. high including funnel.
It had 'paddles' to assist traction.

In the early days of farm machinery, steam engines provided the power
for threshing corn, pumping water and sawing timber. To be moved from
one farm to the next, these engines were mounted on wheeled platforms
and pulled by horses. Then someone hit on the idea of passing a chain
from the engine to one of the wheels so the machine could drive itself. The
traction engine was invented. Boydell's Traction Engine was remarkable
because it had wooden 'paddles' fixed to the wheels to prevent the whole
machine from sinking into the mud.
Unfortunately these floats were so heavy that they were always falling off
and this model was not in service for very long. Nowadays this principle
is used for the caterpillar tracks on numerous vehicles—including those
for farm use. Traction engines themselves remained in use until well into
the 20th century, although by then wheels had been broadened con-
siderably to overcome the problem of mud.

AVELING'S STEAMROLLER 1867

Country: Great Britain. **Size** approx. 20 ft. long, 30 tons.
It was one of the first steamrollers.

Another machine which owes its existence to the steam engine is the
steamroller, which is still in use today for making and repairing roads.
Thanks to the invention of the steamroller, the terrible state of 19th
century roads was vastly improved and damage to the horses' hooves
greatly reduced. A farmer called Thomas Aveling made his first experi-
mental steamroller in 1865. The model in the picture was made in 1867
by his company, Aveling and Porter (which is now called Aveling and
Barford and still manufactures roadmaking machinery). It was bought
by the City of Liverpool and was in regular use in spite of the fact that it
was almost twice as heavy as was necessary (other models weighed only
about 17 tons). The water tank over the front roller held 500 gallons and,
despite the bulk of the machine, it could turn in its own length. You can
see the light wooden wheel, rather like that of a ship, which operated the
chain-driven steering.

RUDGE ORDINARY BICYCLE 1884

Country: Great Britain. **Size:** front wheel 4 ft. 10 in., rear wheel 16 in., and 21½ lbs.
It was one of the earliest bicycles.

The conditions of road surfaces greatly improved after the introduction of the steamroller. As the surfaces became smoother all sorts of vehicles were invented. The bicycle would seem to us a simple invention, yet it did not come into use until the mid-19th century. The type of machine shown here was called an Ordinary, although its shape seems anything but ordinary. It soon became known as a Penny Farthing, from the two coins in current use at the time (the farthing being a quarter of the penny in size). The Rudge Ordinary was exceptionally light even though it had solid rubber tires; and surprisingly the pedals were of a modern 'rat trap' type.

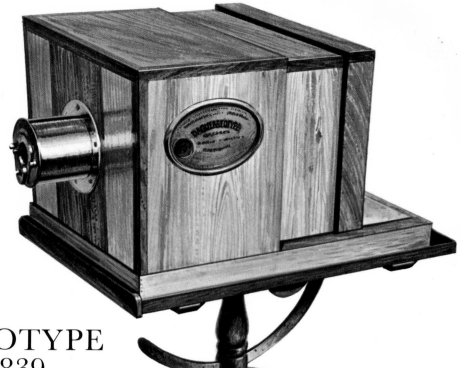

DAGUERROTYPE CAMERA 1839

Country: France. **Size:** 12 in. high, $14\frac{1}{2}$ in. wide, 20 in. long.
It was the first camera to be sold to the public.

From the quality of the first photographs, it is hard to believe that they were made as long ago as 1825 by a Frenchman, Nicephore Niepce. Shortly afterwards the painter Louis Daguerre, another Frenchman, worked with Niepce until he died; then Daguerre began to work alone. This Daguerrotype was the very first camera to be sold to the general public. Each one had a plaque on its side with a guarantee signed by Daguerre himself. There was no shutter apart from the movable lense cover and, since exposure could take up to 40 minutes, a tripod was essential. Shaky hands would have been useless with this camera.

SOLAR PRINTING PRESS 1882

Country: France. **Size:** mirror 10 ft. in diameter.
It was a printing press operated by the heat of the sun.

This printing press is one of the most ingenious attempts to make use of the sun's energy. A cylindrical steam boiler was placed in the center of a curved mirror, measuring 10 feet in diameter. When the mirror was turned towards the sun, the reflected rays generated steam to drive the small 0.4 h.p. engine, which then drove a Marconi printing press. The inventor, a Frenchman, Abel Pifre, demonstrated it in Paris in August 1882.

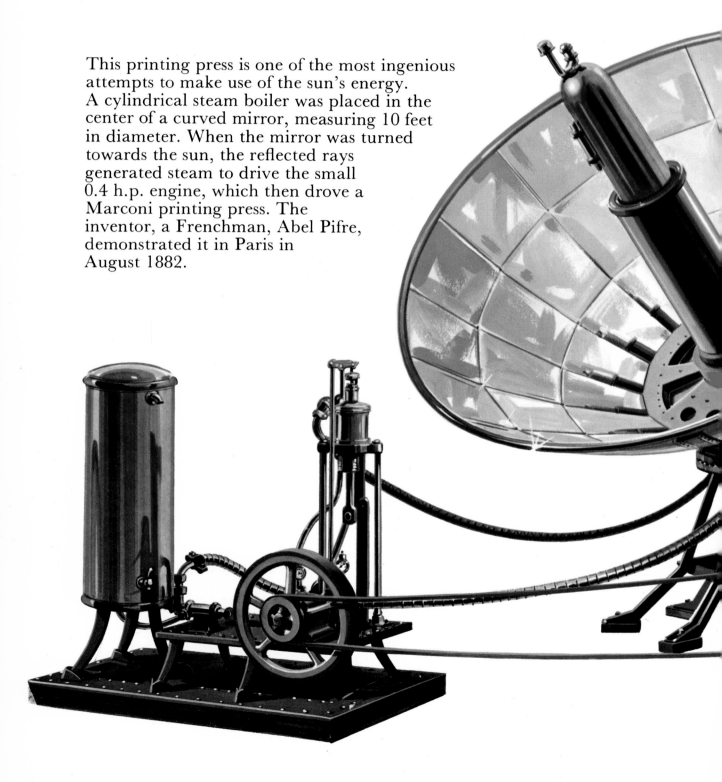

Although on the test day the sun was not very strong, the press operated continuously from 1:00 p.m. to 5:30 p.m. About 500 copies per hour were printed of a journal specially published for the occasion and aptly named the 'Sun-Journal.' Unfortunately this brilliant idea went almost unnoticed and it does seem surprising that this idea was not developed further for use in warm countries.

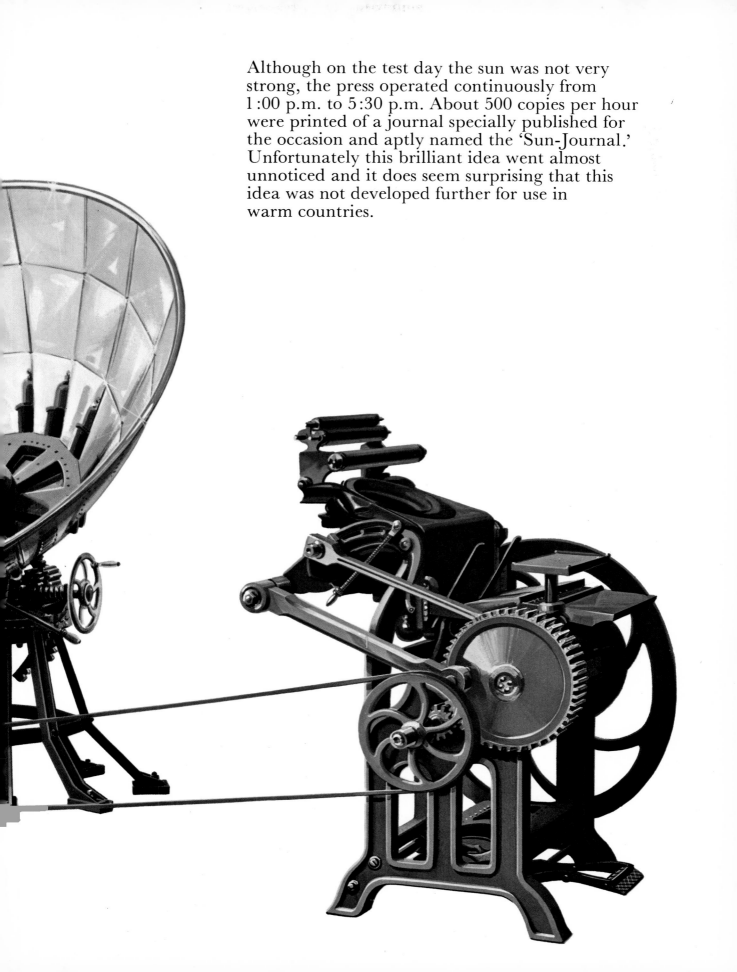

ELECTRIC SEARCHLIGHT 1886

Country: France. **Size:** approx. 10 ft. high, mirror 1 ft. in diameter.
It was the first electric searchlight used for warfare.

Although experiments with electricity date back as far as 1800, electricity for lighting purposes was almost unheard of until the second half of the 19th century, and did not become commonplace until the 20th century. Not surprisingly, the introduction of this first electric searchlight in 1886 caused a sensation. Consisting of a steam engine and dynamo, an electric arc lamp produced a beam that could light objects up to a distance of one mile away. The light itself could be moved in any direction and the whole machine could be drawn by a single horse. Its efficiency and maneuverability made it ideally suited to military purposes.

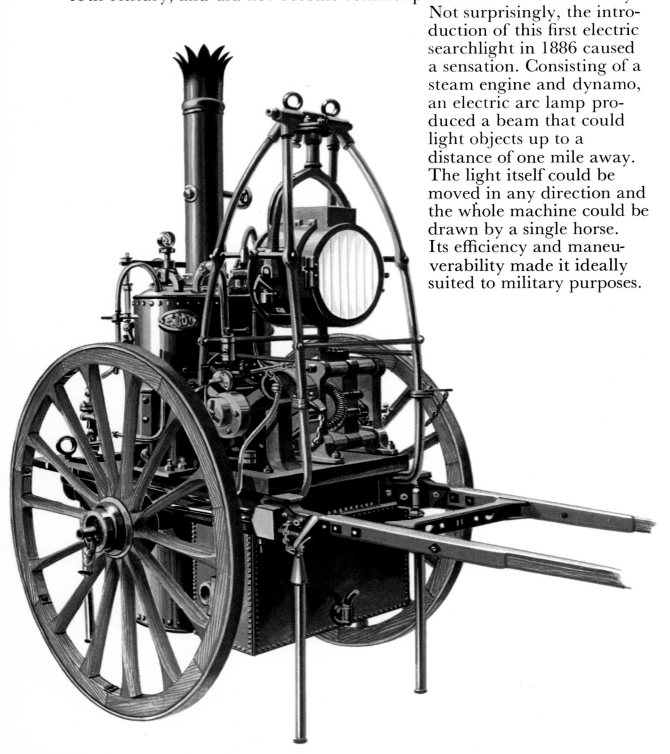

MOLDACOT
POCKET SEWING MACHINE 1885

Country: Germany. **Size:** 8 in. high.
**It was one of the earliest pocket-size
sewing machines.**

Made by S. A. Rosenthal of Berlin in 1885, this
pocket sewing machine arrived in a metal case
measuring only 8 in. by $2\frac{3}{4}$ in. by $1\frac{1}{2}$ in. Sewing
machines had in fact been invented nearly
a hundred years before but this one was
remarkable because of its very tiny size.
Designed to be clamped to a table, it
is hard to understand why this beautiful
pocket sewing machine, which was so
useful and easy to move, was never
more widely used. Heavy iron
machines were popular in the
second half of the 19th century,
and only recently has the trend
been towards smaller,
lightweight models.

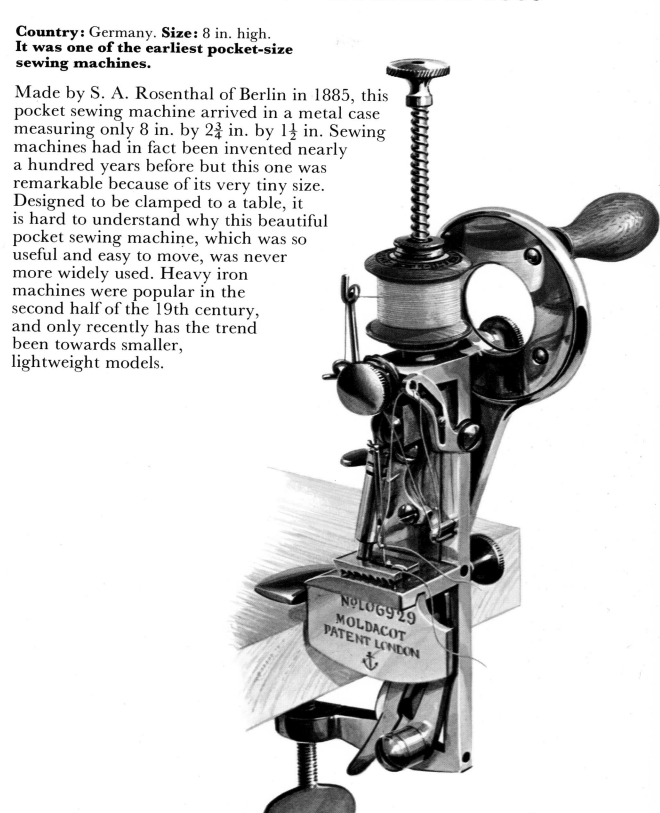

SNOWDON MOUNTAIN RAILWAY ENGINE 1896

Country: Switzerland. **Size:** approx. 10 ft. high, approx. 5 ft. wide, 17¾ tons.
It has been in use for more than 70 years.

At first glance this engine may not look different from any other. But it runs on a rack-rail system, which was designed by Dr. Roman Abt for steep icy gradients, where a normal engine would get no traction. You can see how a special rack of two toothed rails are laid between the normal rails. Beneath the engine are two geared cogwheels, whose teeth engage with those of the rack, thus controlling traction and braking. Mainly used in mountainous countries like Switzerland and Austria, there is only one rack-rail system in Great Britain—the Snowdon Mountain Railway. Opened in 1896 on the day after Easter, this railway still uses four of the original five Swiss-built engines to take tourists up Mount Snowdon.

BERLINER'S GRAMOPHONE 1889

Country: Germany. **Size:** base 8½ in. long, 5⅝ in. wide, 11⅞ in. high (to tip of horn). **It was the first gramophone.**

The first talking machine was constructed by Thomas Edison in 1877. But the first machine that could reproduce musical notes from a disc was the gramophone, invented by a German, Emile Berliner, who emigrated to America. You can see how the turntable was operated by hand and how the large needle picked up the grooves on the specially coated zinc disc. The recording on the disc was transmitted and amplified by the large horn. Remarkably, Berliner's gramophone —the forerunner of today's stereo and hifi equipment— was first put on the market in Germany as a children's toy.

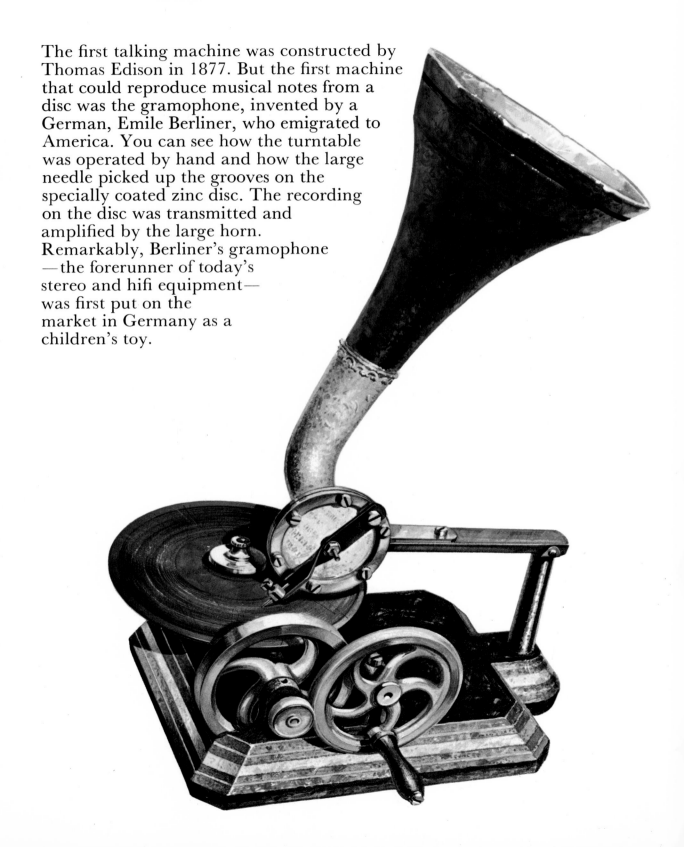

MOOG SYNTHESIZER (MINI-MOOG) 1964

Country: United States. **Size:** approx. 3 ft. long.
It reproduces electronic music.

What could be more of a contrast than the squeaky sounds of the first gramophone compared with the very latest development in electronic music making? Dr. Robert A. Moog, a Dutchman living in the United States, has perfected an instrument which produces electronic music. This is an entirely new sound which has swept the world in the last few years. Moog describes his synthesizer as 'basically a solo instrument like a violin or clarinet,' but the sound it produces is nothing like either. It has entirely revolutionized modern music, written by both serious composers and pop groups. Although started as gimmicks for TV commercials, electronic sounds are now used more and more in the introductions to TV and radio programs.

ELECTRON MICROSCOPE 1972

Country: Great Britain. **Size:** 2 ft. 10 in. wide, 4 ft. 1 in. high.
It is one of the most powerful microscopes.

A Dutchman, Zacharias Jansen, invented the first microscope and man could see things that before had been too small for his eye to see, even with the help of a magnifying glass. Now, 500 years later, the EM 201 High Resolution Electron Microscope magnifies objects by 200,000 times their actual size. This close examination of plant and animal life through such microscopes has enabled scientists to begin to solve the mysteries of nature that have been on earth for thousands of years. It is hard to believe that such a powerful microscope is contained in one unit no larger than an average office desk.

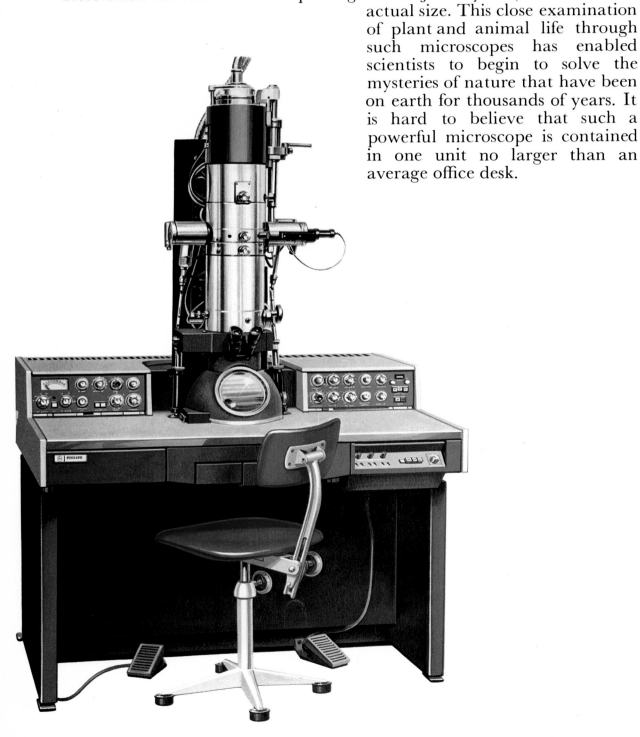

ZEISS UNIVERSAL PROJECTOR 1953

Country: West Germany. **Size:** 17 ft. high and 2 tons.
It can project an exact replica of the universe.

Some 2,500 years ago the ancient Greeks made models of the universe revolving around the earth. In 1919 Professor Bauersfeld, chief engineer of the Carl Zeiss Co., invented the first projection planetarium from which this universal projector was developed. The picture illustrates how this extraordinary machine has about 150 separate projectors which throw images of 8,900 stars and planets onto the inside of a large dome. Sitting inside the dome, you can see an exact replica of the sky as it would appear at any time of the year.

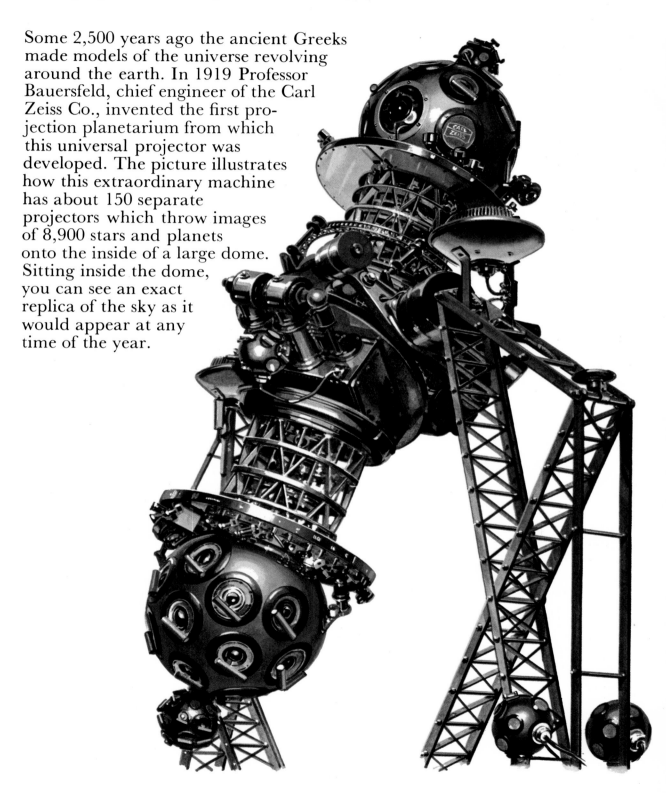

JODRELL BANK
RADIO TELESCOPE 1957

Country: Great Britain. **Size:** bowl 250 ft. in diameter, overall weight: 2,000 tons.
It can look into the skies.

While some scientists are concerned with the study of life on earth,
others are examining outer space to find out more about the stars
and planets. The invention of the telescope greatly helped early
scientists, and the more powerful the lenses became, the greater
the number of stars that were discovered. Today's radio
telescopes with their fantastic range have led to some of
the most exciting discoveries about the universe.
The Jodrell Bank Radio Telescope at Cheshire, England,
has a bowl measuring 250 feet in diameter and weighing
750 tons. The early telescopes worked by
reflecting light by means of glass lenses, but
the radio telescope collects radio waves. The
one at Jodrell Bank can 'look' into the skies
1,000 times farther than an optical telescope.
It is used to penetrate the distant universe,
and is able to track natural or man-made
objects automatically through the sky.
It was used to track the orbit of the
first Sputnik and has since been
used for numerous further probes.

WHITTLE JET ENGINE 1937

Country: Great Britain. **Size:** 4½ ft. long, 2 ft. high.
It was the first gas turbine jet engine.

When you blow up a toy balloon and then let go, the air
rushing out in one direction makes the balloon fly off the
opposite way. Sir Frank Whittle (then Flight-Lieutenant
Whittle) began experiments in about 1928, hoping to use
this principle to produce a more powerful engine for airplanes. A few years later, he produced his first gas turbine jet
propulsion engine, the principles of which remain the same
today. Fans suck in air, which is compressed and then com-
bined with fuel. When this mixture is ignited, it is expelled
through turbines under such pressure that it creates the
forward thrust—just like the balloon. By the beginning of
World War II, Whittle's small firm was hard at work pro-
ducing engines for Britain's first jet airplanes. Germany
was also developing the jet engine and, by the end of the war,
both countries had jet fighters in service.
Although developed for air-
planes, the jet engine is
now used for ships,
trucks and power
stations.

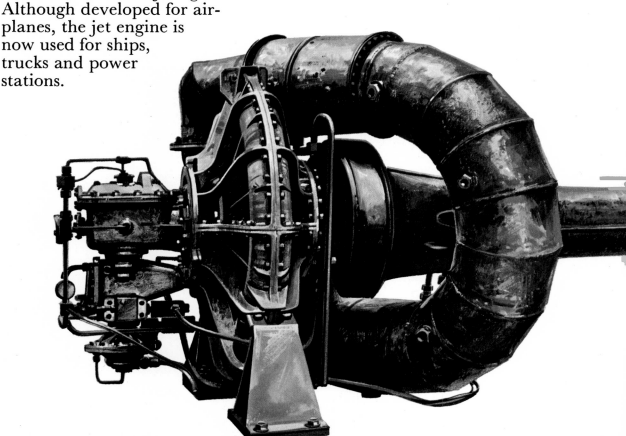

FLYING
BEDSTEAD 1954

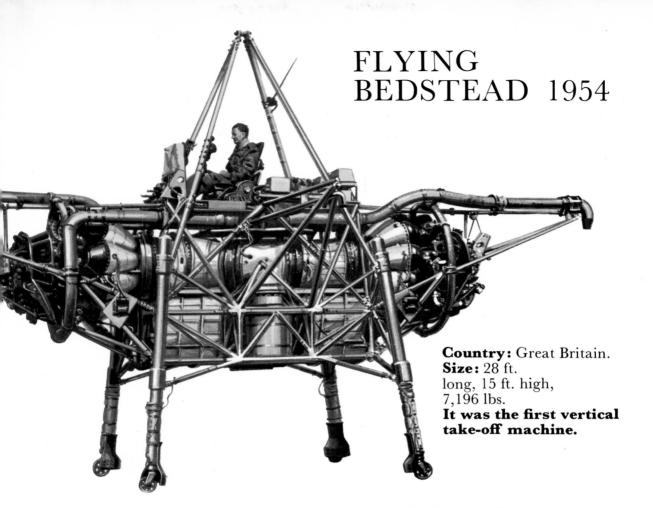

Country: Great Britain.
Size: 28 ft.
long, 15 ft. high,
7,196 lbs.
**It was the first vertical
take-off machine.**

The faster the speed of take-off, the more the
danger is increased. The difficulty in finding
suitable space and the constant striving for
greater safety has led to new ideas in aviation.
Dr. A. A. Griffith, who worked at Rolls Royce,
began experimenting with the idea of using jet
engines to lift planes up off the ground.
This first vertical take-off machine was a test
rig, which, because of the way it looked, soon
became known as The Flying Bedstead. It was
made of a tubular frame on four legs with two
Rolls Royce Nene turbojet engines mounted
back to back.
With no wings and an awkward appearance,
the Flying Bedstead was completely successful.
Since then there have been a number of
successful vertical take-off aircraft, including
the French Mirage and British Harrier fighters.

LUNA I
(also called Lunik) 1959

Country: U.S.S.R. **Size:** weighs approx. 1 ton.
It was the first successful probe to the moon.

Not content with viewing the planets from afar, man's next step was to investigate at close quarters. Lunik I was the first successful probe to the moon and carried a series of scientific instruments and batteries weighing 796 lbs. Launched from the U.S.S.R., it flew past the moon at a distance of about 3,700 miles and disappeared into space, becoming a tiny planet circling endlessly around the sun. Eight months later Lunik 2 crash-landed on the moon's surface and became the first man-made object to reach another world. Within a month another probe, Lunik 3, sent back to earth the first photograph of the far side of the moon.

SATURN V ROCKET 1969

Country: United States. **Size:** 363 ft. high and 3,000 tons.
It was the first spacecraft to land a man on the moon.

While the Russians were working on machines to explore
the moon's surface, scientists in America were
designing a spacecraft which would fulfil man's
greatest dream: to land a man on the moon.
This spacecraft was called Apollo II. In this
picture you can see the enormously powerful
Saturn V rocket which sent the craft on its
mammoth voyage. The rocket is built in three
stages which fall away when burned out.
Burning 15 tons of fuel every second, the
first stage lasts only 2 minutes 40
seconds. By the time the third stage
is reached, the craft is travelling
towards the moon at a speed of
24,700 miles per hour. The
journey of Apollo II and the
landing of Neil Armstrong,
the first man to set foot on
the moon, is perhaps the
most historic event of
all time.

LUNOKHOD I 1970

Country: U.S.S.R. **Weight:** 1,667 lbs.
It was the first robot to land on the moon.

A new age of space exploration was opened when the U.S.S.R. first landed a robot on the moon. When Luna 17 was launched, the announcement that it was 'to continue exploration of the moon' gave no hint to the western world that inside this rocket was a machine undreamed of even in science fiction. After a perfect soft landing on the moon, the craft put out ramps at either side and a strange-looking, eight-wheeled robot slowly rolled down to the moon's surface. Driven by remote control, it was directed by a TV/radio link from a center in the heart of the U.S.S.R. Because of the moon's uneven surface, Lunokhod's wheels were made of woven wire with titanium plates, and a cutout mechanism enabled it to move on even if only two wheels on each side were working. For nearly a year Lunokhod crawled over the moon's surface, making more than 500 studies of soil and sending back more than 20,000 pictures of the lunar surface. Also on board were a panoramic camera and X-ray equipment which could examine remote parts of the universe.

GLOSSARY

cogwheel: (geared) wheel with projecting teeth that transfers motion and drives another similar wheel. If the cogwheels are of unequal size, the speed of motion is altered, and they are said to be geared.

dynamo: machine that generates electricity.

exposure: time taken for film to be subjected to light.

flintlock: mechanism for firing gun. Flint produces spark to ignite powder and fire shot.

gears: combination of wheels which engage with each other to alter drive speed.

to ignite: heat to the point at which substance starts to burn.

Industrial Revolution: changes to industry brought about in the late 18th and early 19th centuries by the introduction of mechanical inventions.

magazine: container attached to gun and holding supply of ammunition.

projector: apparatus for casting rays of light and forming images on surfaces.

rat trap pedals: cycle pedals made of two parallel iron plates with teeth.

remote control: control of apparatus from a point some distance away by means of electrically operated device.

robot: a machine controlled by an electrically operated device from a point some distance away.

shutter: control that is opened and closed to allow lens of camera to be exposed to the light for a specific time.

traction engine: self-propelled steam engine used to pull heavy loads.

tripod: stool or table resting on three legs used to support camera.